Date Due

Canoe Tripping with Kids

Canoe Tripping with Kids

David and Judy Harrison

Drawings by NANCY HARRISON

The Stephen Greene Press • *Brattleboro, Vermont*

With thanks to Christopher Merrill for his help and encouragement and to Shirley Olson for her work on the manuscript. Our greatest debt is to Charles H. and Huntington W., our own mentors.

Produced in the UNITED STATES OF AMERICA.
Designed by DOUGLAS KUBACH.
Published by THE STEPHEN GREENE PRESS,
Fessenden Road, Brattleboro, Vermont 05301.

Library of Congress Cataloging in Publication Data

HARRISON, DAVID, 1938–
  Canoe tripping with kids.

  Includes bibliographical references and index.
  1. Canoes and canoeing.   2. Family recreation.
I. HARRISON, JUDY, 1939–   joint author.   II. Title.
GV789.H37   797.1'22   80-28213
ISBN 0-8289-0426-X (pbk.)

FRONTISPIECE: Black Lake, Saskatchewan, at sunset.

"Ye who love the haunts of Nature,
Love the sunshine of the meadow,
Love the wind among the branches,
And the rain-shower and the snowstorm
And the rushing of great rivers
Through their palisades of pine trees,
And the thunder in the mountains,
Whose innumerable echoes
Flap like eagles in their eyries; . . ."

SONG OF HIAWATHA

To you who dream of sharing this with your
children, we dedicate this book.